Everybody
Works

Everybody
Works

Shelley Rotner and Ken Kreisler

Photographs by Shelley Rotner

M Millbrook Press • Minneapolis

To my parents — who are always working. — Shelley

For Linda, Sami, Kara, and Crackies who
never stop working at making my life complete. — Ken

Text copyright © 2003 by Shelley Rotner and Ken Kreisler
Photographs copyright © 2003 by Shelley Rotner
Reprinted in 2006

Millbrook Press, Inc.
A division of Lerner Publishing Group
241 First Avenue North
Minneapolis, Minnesota 55401 U.S.A.
Website address: www.lernerbooks.com

Library of Congress Cataloging-in-Publication Data

Rotner, Shelley.
Everybody works / Shelley Rotner and Ken Kreisler;
photographs by Shelley Rotner.
p. cm.
Summary: Photographs and simple text show
the many ways in which work can be accomplished.
ISBN-13: 978-0-7613-1751-7 (lib. bdg. : alk. paper)
ISBN-10: 0-7613-1751-1 (lib. bdg. : alk. paper)
1. Work—Pictorial works—Juvenile literature. 2. Occupations—Pictorial works—
Juvenile literature. 3. Professions—Pictorial works—Juvenile literature.
4. Vocational guidance—Pictorial works—Juvenile literature. [1. Work—Pictorial works.
2. Occupations—Pictorial works.] I. Kreisler, Ken. II. Title.
HD4902.5 .R67 2003
306.3′6—dc21
2002009045

Manufactured in the United States of America
2 3 4 5 6 7 — DP — 11 10 09 08 07 06

Everybody works in different ways.

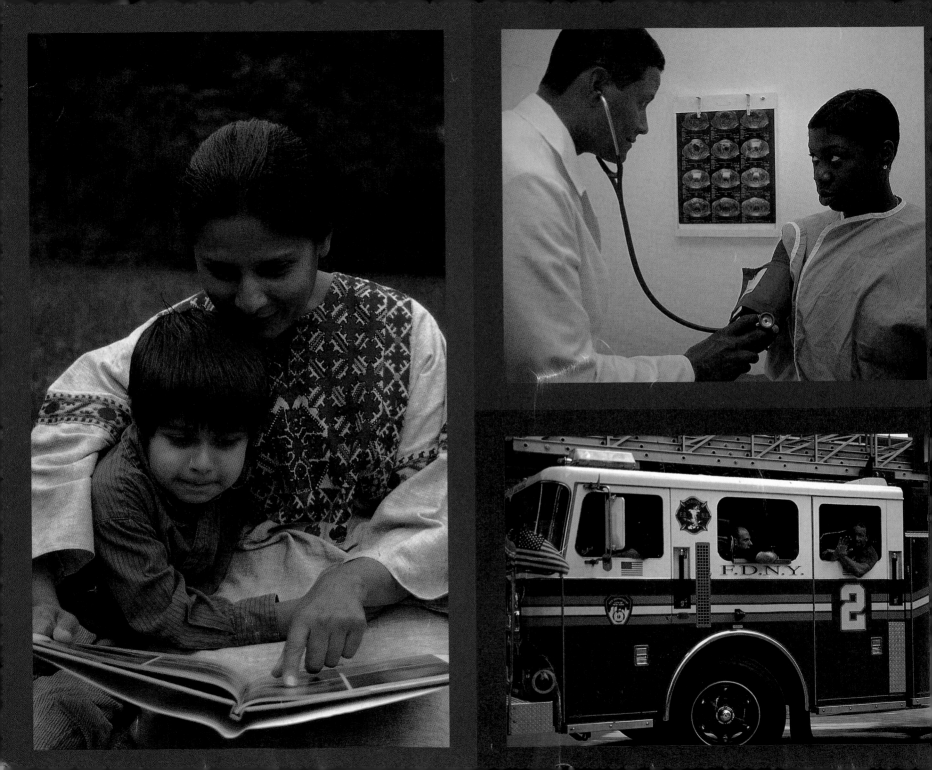

Work is caring
and protecting.

Work is
delivering
and selling.

Work is creating,

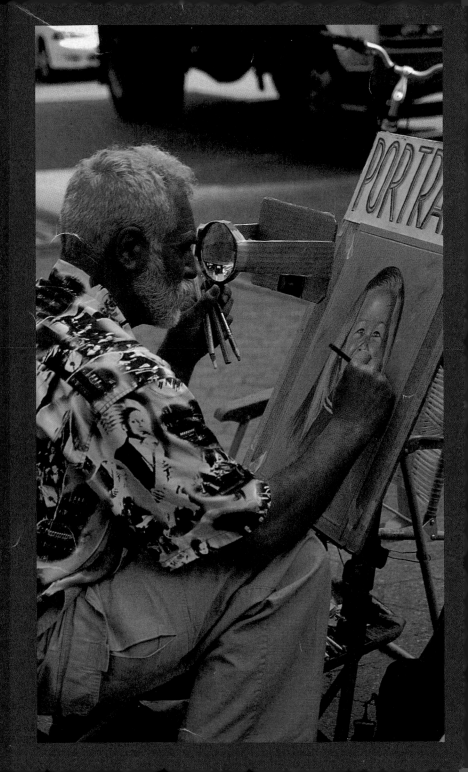

**and building,
and fixing.**

Some people
make things.

Some people grow things,
or cook the food we eat.

Some work in an office.

Some work at home.

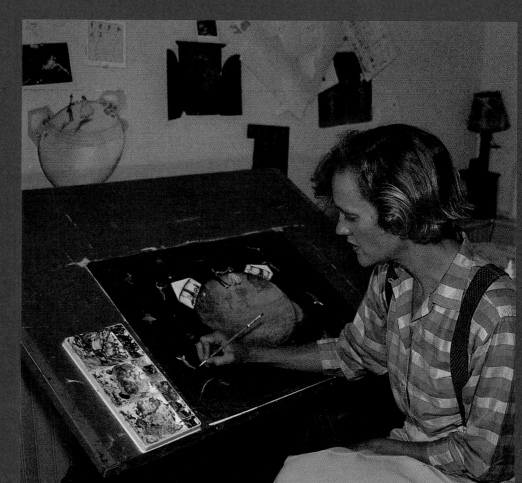

Others work outside,

or travel from
place to place.

**Some work
to earn money,**

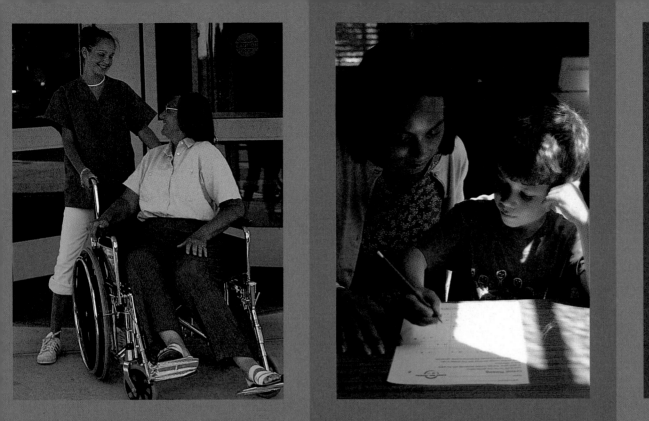

**or volunteer
because they
are needed.**

Sometimes work is
a hobby—just for fun.

Children work, too.

Even animals work.

Everybody works.
What about you?